VICTORIA

Damian Harvey

Illustrated by Rupert Van Wyk

W

Contents

CHAPTER 1
Young Heiress

When Victoria was born on 24th
May 1819 in Kensington Palace, the
royal family were not very popular.
Her grandfather, George III, was still
King and lots of relatives were in
line for the throne.

No one thought Victoria would ever
become Queen…

…but then things started to change.

Before Victoria's first birthday, her father, Prince Edward the Duke of Kent, caught pneumonia and died. Six days later, her grandfather died and her uncle, George IV, became King.

Victoria lived in Kensington Palace with her mother, but they weren't very rich. Most of the carpets were thin and worn and they couldn't afford fine food.

Victoria spent most of her time playing on her own with her dolls.

Uncle Frederick, the Duke of York, died in 1827. Three years later, King George IV died. William IV was crowned King and suddenly 11 year-old Victoria found herself next in line to the throne.

I wonder how long this one will last!

Victoria's mother made sure that the young princess would be well prepared for the time she would become Queen.

For a start, Victoria was the first royal child to be vaccinated against smallpox – a disease that had almost killed Queen Elizabeth I.

Instead of going to school, Victoria had her lessons at the palace. She loved singing and drawing. Her mother gave her a diary that she wrote in every day.

The young princess wanted to
see how other people lived so she
travelled around the country and
wrote about everything she saw.

Victoria made up her mind to try
and make things better when she
became Queen – and she wouldn't
have long to wait.

CHAPTER 2
The New Queen

On 20th June 1837, Victoria's mother woke her up and told her the Archbishop of Canterbury and Lord Conyngham wanted to see her.

After putting on her dressing-gown, the young princess went to see the two men waiting for her in the sitting room.

There, they gave her the sad news that her uncle, King William IV, had died.

Lord Conyngham knelt before her, kissed her hand and told her that she was now Queen.

11

When Victoria was crowned Queen at Westminster Abbey, thousands of people came to London to see her. Everyone cheered as the procession went by. Not everything went well...

…The Archbishop put Victoria's coronation ring on the wrong finger.

Old Lord Rolle fell down the stairs as he tried to kiss the royal crown.

Then there was a mad rush when medals were thrown into the air.

Some people worried that Victoria was too young to be Queen. They thought she wouldn't be able to rule the country – but they were wrong. Victoria was stubborn and bold.

She moved to Buckingham Palace so she could get away from her mother and be more independent.

She liked the Prime Minister, Lord Melbourne, and often asked him for advice. She even asked for advice on who to marry.

Lord Melbourne made a list of suitable husbands but Victoria wanted to marry someone she loved.

CHAPTER 3
Wedding Bells

When Prince Albert, Victoria's German cousin, came to visit the palace in 1839, she fell head over heals in love with him.

Queen Victoria didn't waste any time. Five days later, she asked Prince Albert to marry her.

It was the happiest moment of Victoria's life when her handsome prince said yes.

Victoria and Albert were married
on 10th February 1840 at St James's
Palace. Thousands of people filled
the streets to watch them pass by –
even though it rained all day.

The Queen wore a beautiful white dress for her wedding day, a fashion that has continued to this day. Prince Albert dressed in a smart, British Field Marshall's uniform.

When their first child, Victoria (Vicky) was born, the Queen and Prince Albert decided they didn't want servants to look after her. Albert decided that he should look after the children while Victoria looked after the country.

They had nine children altogether, and their second child, Albert (Bertie), would one day be King... even though he was always getting up to mischief.

Victoria and Albert loved getting away from the hustle and bustle of royal life. They spent lots of time at Osborne House on the Isle of Wight where they loved going to the beach.

They bought an old castle at Balmoral in Scotland and dressed up like normal people so no one would recognise them.

At Christmas they decorated a fir tree with candles. They also sent cards to friends and family through the post. The first stamps were known as Penny Blacks and they had a picture of the Queen's head on them.

CHAPTER 4
Changing World

Life wasn't always peaceful.

In 1845 a great famine struck Ireland and over a million people starved. Many more left the country in search of somewhere else to live.

Victoria donated a lot of money to help, but people that didn't like her called her the Famine Queen.

A few people tried to assassinate Victoria as she passed by in her carriage. Luckily, they weren't very good shots.

One man even managed to hit her with his stick before being arrested.

Britain was changing very quickly. There were new developments in science and technology.

Isambard Kingdom Brunel helped Britain to progress. He built railways, tunnels and bridges to make it easier to travel.

He also designed a huge ship called the *Great Britain*. It was made from metal instead of wood, and powered by a propeller instead of wind or oars.

It was the first modern ship and, at the time, it was the biggest ever built. Prince Albert launched the *Great Britain* in 1843.

In 1851 Queen Victoria opened
the Great Exhibition at the Crystal
Palace in London. Inside were
displays of the latest goods from
the British Empire. There were steam
engines, spinning machines, fine art,
jewellery and lots more.

Millions of people from around the
world went to see the exhibition.
Even famous writers like Charles
Dickens and Charlotte Bronte
came to see it.

Not all was going well for Britain. British soldiers were fighting in the Crimean War against Russia. Lots of soldiers died from wounds and diseases until nurses, such as Florence Nightingale, went to help.

Other nurses such as Mary Seacole also helped save the lives of many soldiers. Queen Victoria wrote to thank her – even though she didn't think it was the right kind of work for a woman.

To reward the bravery of the soldiers, she created the Victoria Cross medal.

The Queen was delighted when their daughter, Vicky, married Prince Frederick. He was heir to the throne of Prussia, a large part of the German Kingdom.

She was even happier when they had a baby. Victoria was a grandmother at the age of 39.

But then disaster struck. Prince Albert became very ill. The doctors thought he had typhoid fever. There was nothing they could do to help.

The Prince died two weeks later at the age of 42. Victoria was devastated.

From that day on, Queen Victoria only wore black clothes to show how sad she was at the loss of her beloved Albert.

And she was determined that others would remember him too. The Royal Albert Hall was built and named after him. So was the Albert Memorial in Hyde Park and the Albert Embankment on the River Thames.

CHAPTER 5
Getting Old

Victoria missed Albert so much that she found it hard to carry on being Queen. Her mother had died the year before and most of her government friends were dead too.

The Queen spent a lot of time riding in Scotland and people hardly saw her for years.

Victoria's best friend was a Scottish servant called John Brown. She trusted John and often asked him for advice but people teased her about her friendship with a servant.

Victoria still had to work with the Prime Ministers, though she didn't always like them, especially William Gladstone. Her powers as Queen were changing too. The Government took more decisions.

He's so boring!

Her favourite Prime Minister was Benjamin Disraeli. He flattered Victoria and tried to make her happy.

It was Disraeli that finally persuaded Victoria to come back into public life. He said that she should be made the Empress of India, the largest country in the British Empire.

Victoria loved India, even though she never went there. She thought it would be much too hot.

She had an Indian advisor called Abdul Karim who taught her Hindustani and helped her with Indian business.

It's the jewel in my crown.

By 1897, Victoria had been Queen for 60 years and she was the most famous monarch in the world.

Her Golden Jubilee was celebrated across the whole Empire. There were parades and parties and souvenirs.

As she got older, Victoria didn't want to show any signs of weakness. She still rode around in her open carriage, even when it was raining.

In 1899, a war began in South Africa between the Boers, Dutch-speaking farmers, and the British Army. People called it the Boer War.

To help keep her soldiers happy, Victoria sent them 100,000 tins of chocolate. Each tin was decorated with a picture of Victoria's face.

Queen Victoria died on 22nd January 1901, a year before the war was over. She had reigned for longer than any other British monarch. She was the first queen to be photographed and to have toilets in all her homes. During her reign, the British Empire had become the biggest in the world.

As her funeral procession went by, thousands of people silently lined the streets of London. Everyone wanted to catch a final glimpse of their much loved, long-serving Queen.

45

Timeline

1819   24th May: Victoria is born at Kensington Palace, London.

1820   Victoria's father, Prince Edward, dies and she becomes heir to the throne.

1837   20th June: King William IV dies and Vicoria becomes Queen.

1838   Queen Victoria's coronation at Westminster Abbey, London.

1840   Queen Victoria marries Prince Albert at St James's Palace.

1845	Potato famine in Ireland.
1851	Victoria opens the Great Exhibition in Hyde Park.
1854	The Crimean War against Russia starts.
1861	Prince Albert dies of typhoid.
1871	Victoria opens the Royal Albert Hall in memory of her husband.
1897	Victoria's Diamond Jubilee.
1899	The Boer War starts in South Africa.
1901	22nd January: Queen Victoria dies after 64 years on the throne.

First published in 2014 by
Franklin Watts
338 Euston Road
London NW1 3BH

Franklin Watts Australia
Level 17/207 Kent Street
Sydney NSW 2000

HB ISBN 978 1 4451 3313 3
PB ISBN 978 14451 3314 0
Library ebook ISBN 978 1 4451 3316 4
ebook ISBN 978 1 4451 3309 6

Dewey Decimal Classification Number: 941'.081'092

Series editor: Melanie Palmer
Series designer Cathryn Gilbert

Printed and bound by CPI Group (UK) Ltd, CR0 4YY

Franklin Watts is a division of Hachette Children's Books,
an Hachette UK company.
www.hachette.co.uk